Never Far from the Egg Harbor Ice House

Never Far from the Egg Harbor Ice House

Poems

John Repp

Sheila-Na-Gig Editions

Cover photo: Edward Karl Repp, 1917
Author photo: Katherine Knupp

ISBN: 978-1-962405-50-8
Library of Congress Control Number: 2025950634

Sheila-Na-Gig Editions
Russell, KY
Hayley Mitchell Haugen, Editor
www.sheilanagigblog.com

Acknowledgments

Thanks to editors who made homes for versions of these poems:

Adirondack Review: "Civil Service, Soldiers' Home"
ArLiJo: "'The Last Time I Went Fishing Was the Last Time We Went Fishing'"
Bitterzoet Magazine: "Ice Cream Sandwich"
Cobalt: "Names & Places"
Crab Orchard Review: "The Salt Hay"
Door is Ajar: "Shimmy Shimmy Ko-Ko-Bop"
failbetter: "Some Random Issues"
Foliate Oak: "Poem Beginning With a Line From Fernando Pessoa"
The Furious Gazelle: "Horticulture"
Gasher Journal: "Ode to Newspapers Big as Pizza Boxes"
The Hamilton Stone Review: "After Driving Through the Holland Tunnel" and "The Arc of a Life"
Handsy: "Oh, Those Summer Mornings in the Days of Empire"
Ink in Thirds: "Another Naïve Poem"
Lake Effect: "Beets"
Mayday: "UHF Ode"
Oyster River Pages: "Merit Badge"
Poetrybay: "Convenient Worms" and "What Lola Means to Me"
Red Ochre Lit: "Hook & Release"
Rune: "They Could Have Had Something"
Slant: "Milk"
Smeuse Poetry (UK): "Breakfast at the Woodstown Diner"
Smoky Blue Literary and Arts Magazine: "Driving Home" and "Say *Yo!*"
Spry Literary Journal: "The Invention of Gunpowder"
Variant Literature: "In the Pines"
Vine Leaves Literary Journal (Australia): "Apollo"
The Waiting Room: "Plans"
whimperbang: "October Cold Rain Refusing"

"Hook & Release" was reprinted in *Cold-Running Current*, a chapbook published by Alice Greene & Co.

"In the Pines" was reprinted in *Star Shine in the Pines*, a chapbook published by Seven Kitchens Press.

To be at home in the world we need to keep it inhospitable.

Adam Phillips

Contents

I

II

III

IV

I

Burn Barrel

Halloween meant trudging through sultry twilight
        along the highway to the house behind the florist's
to the one by the awning place to the concrete-block cube

        among the chicken coops to Vince's Auto for Vince's
caramel apples to the trailer park where the 1956 Bel-Air
        our grandmother still drove to Vertolli's, A & P, Siloam

& every birthday gleamed in the ambient light of her metal home.
        The juiciest pear of high culture could never out-sweeten
the thick air's liquor. In full dark, The Mummy, Mandrake

        & Casper the Friendly Ghost dragged pillowcases crammed
with easy candy home. The burn barrel glowed on the slab
        our father had poured not a month before. Not Proust

nor Goya could render the sublimity of the leaf piles tended
        by raking silhouettes that fumed along the highway
from Santini's Lunch to the air strip where crop-dusters—

        biplanes more defiantly fragile than any Ravel a flautist
could waft through Symphony Hall—sat humped beneath tarps.
        A Midsummer Night's Dream in Edith Wharton's back yard

or a single whiff of skunk cabbage dying back another year?
The door between the worlds has always stood open.

Convenient Worms

filled the behemoth cooler on the fresh
concrete slab next to the burn barrel—coin slot,
crank, stenciled sign extolling price & quality,
chrome receptacle that cradled each boughten
waxed cylinder inside which two dozen
night crawlers shone in peaty dark.

Imagine the proprietor pulling up in the rare,
crisp dusk of a summer day spent rolling
past the first split-levels on their beveled plots
then veering southeast to the lighthouse,
the concrete elephant & the Palace Depression
miraculously not crumbling into its constituent

glass shards, marbles & Progresso soup cans
then north for ice cream, the family plump
& quiet in the lull of rumbly wheels paid for
in part by the slick worms gone forth now
to die on hooks piercing the lower lips of crappies
& bass & wizened pike with those razor teeth.

Imagine filling your pockets with coins,
your neon name buzzing overhead, the goods
beyond the plate glass mere shadows, a semi
banging past behind you, kids clapping
as they run inside the bungalow whose every
corner-cut flaw you could fix if you just

had the time, wife already running the first
bath as you let the screen door slap shut,
worrying for now about not one thing.

Milk

Every morning, two milk deliveries
because it was good for the business
alive only when I think of it.

In the cellar, a tabby cat plucked
a hind leg from a cricket
so he could bat the bug spinning

on the damp concrete. One milkman
left an amber half-gallon,
the other a quart with a puckered,

thick-lipped mouth. Frigid air
billowed from the bait chest,
piles of squid, blocks of chum,

cardboard cups of brine shrimp
& rafts of bunker frozen
in a single mind. The cat ate

the cricket & caught another.
Every week, a hamster died
in the attic, tears got shed

& another rodent hope got dropped
in the cage to scrabble the wheel
& roast in perpetual August.

Coins jingled in cavernous pockets
where chocolate lived & mints
& tide charts torn from the *Press*

& mollusk shells brought home
from midnight jetties. Imagine it!
Cold milk in the milk box, a thunk

when the cardboard stopper
got tugged out, dew on the glass
in summer, milk cold enough

to pain the teeth, "milk box" alive
in fewer & fewer minds, "milkman"
a vanished misnomer, "the business"

a fifty-year fever & balm, both milkmen
happy customers—Ebner casting squid
off Barnegat Light, Schaeffer drowning worms

in Union Lake, the sinkers & lures & hooks
we greedily drank deep in the mire now.
Ah, the silken sluice of milk in the morning!

UHF Ode

All we can expect from children is the memory the monk
has of the time he was attached.   Adam Gopnik

Saturdays are not what they used to be during my personal Neolithic,
        Sky King & Penny dipping their wings toward the desert floor,
oiled Steve Reeves in the gladiator pit thrilling my brother,

        pith-helmeted Ramar of the Jungle squelching along the fetid
trails of "Darkest Africa" as poison darts zipped by & snakes hissed
        in the sun-swallowing vines. Friend Flicka, gleaming Fury,

oh what heights we hit. *Hey, Rocky! Watch me pull a rabbit out of my hat!*
        Again & again I miss it—not nostalgic, no, the aroma of corn flakes
& Ebner's milk, the patter of rain on the rotting sill, the certainty

        of Larry Ferrari & cinnamon toast for supper & thus this poem
pondering itself, these words not what remain but all that can be done.
        Out the window right now, someone trims grass at the base

of a brick wall, a job I once did with what I now know was love—
        eight months a year, sweaty peace at the sight of smooth,
aromatic green. Years before, my father bolted to the roof an antenna

        rotated with a toggle screwed to a switch plate mounted
by the maroon armchair called "Dad's Chair" though Dad
        rarely sat there. Three new stations in Philly & we had them—

day-long Spanish cowpokes, roller derby live from the Palestra,
        Speed Racer's half-dozen cels, an orgy of Godzillas & mummies,
puppets & giant ants. An age later, Saturdays high-step double-time,

        the only Gigantor the one fattened on breast milk & mashed peas
who thirty post-nuclear seconds later crafts on the kitchen floor a tale
        of aliens & warrior cats. My father should never again climb

a ladder, let alone the dry-rotted thing his father climbed to paint eaves
       & soffit, but does anyway, folding afterward into the weed-plucking,
finch-loving geezer he can't possibly have become. Praise the poem

       gone sentimental! Hike the hills of fatherhood clichés, fetching up
where I stand foursquare between the granite stiles marking our home
       & intone to whomever comes to drag my son to that year's glory

Over my dead body though I'll crunch that day as all days the grit of every
       back-lot Normandy I've ever died on, munching in the immortal dusk
stale bread & sardines—bones & all—as my father taught. Or I swallow

everything as my warrior says *I have to, Papa.*

Hook & Release

Cream Soda in Dividing Creek, 1960

Slap of screen door,
clank of cooler,

dank aroma of smoke,
salt marsh & low tide,

bark & bellow of men,
soft sweetness

of the snack cake.
A coin squeezed

between finger & thumb,
your very own hand

pushing it in & pulling
the bottle free.

His big hand around
yours around the bottle

tugged down, the cap
clattering into the bucket.

Out in the sun to the car,
cold sweet clear fizz

everywhere inside, the aroma
of him & the orange soda

he drinks in three big swallows.

Trout

What to do about the trout?
The trout lilts on the tongue

even inert in the box
it lies in. The trout

is a dilemma, despite the lilt
the fifty-year-old fish

flips each time I purse
my lips to lead to the lilt

the trout inevitably lends
the looming air of rumbly rain

whenever the question comes.
The question always finds

a cool swirl to rest in. The question
will never be hooked & released.

The trout's mildewed tail
curls into the air inside the box.

The rainbow is still the colors
the air can make.

Watercress

The dog stood in the creek
& could not drink. Hot & wet

the air that did not move
as he stood there. He pushed

his tongue out & pulled
it in. He did not yank watercress

from the creek as he many times
had done. Green tendrils undulated

around his haunches. The current
ran cold, even in high summer.

Water Rats

Water rats made wakes
swimming upstream. Nearly long

& sleek as otters, they slipped
up the slick bank to the pile

of shattered concrete for whatever
rat reasons kept them there

till they scrabbled out again.
Often, the dog would snatch one

off the hill. After he died,
I shot them with the .22

I was at last old enough to use.

Damascus

The only dog I ever loved
trotted ahead on the trail

to our secret Damascus.
No salvation on offer

where we ran, no words
or worries, the Blackwater's

swish & burble under
the rotting bridge joy enough

for what time we had.

One Day

One day, the dog
lay in the scrub oak's shade

& died. I dug a hole
& dragged him in.

I don't care what Paul thought
about animal souls. I belong

to no congregation
& pray only in despair

& fury. Ticks infest
those woods, but not yet these—

leaf-litter ankle-deep,
slate sky, mallards bobbing

in the lagoon. The dog
glances back now & then,

leading me where I go.

Plans

After the salesman had gone,
        under the fluorescent ring
                buzzing like a hoarse child,

shrouded in the fume
        of a fresh cigarette, our father
                mulled the bomb shelter

we could maybe think about
        affording—schematics,
                easy payment plans,

reputable local contractors,
        two of whom he'd known
                since second grade—& doodled

us five inside the design
        that looked best, but my God,
                even spread out over ten

or fifteen years, the cost
        of concrete & steel alone
                could double our bungalow's

footprint on the fill
        a builder would need
                to test for sufficient

density—& the supplies!
        For how long? Three kids
                with nothing to do? *Hon, we don't*

have to, our mother said,
        resting one cheek on a fist,
                the three of us itching

to go watch TV. He'd planned,
      post-holed, sawn, shoveled,
            hammered, raked, pipe-wrenched

& bolted everything
      but the house itself,
            none of which would

come home to us till long
      after—how to put it?
            My father's hands

knotted & unknotted near
      an iron sink piled with pots
            & plates sixty years ago,

the rockets & jets
      aimed at every last "us"
            permanent as lust.

The Arc of a Life

I've said *the arc of a life*
more in the past month
than in the rest of my life

so far & with good luck
in what days remain. A boy
in his first brogans squints

at the camera, fists thrust
in his Sunday knickers.
In Jesus' name, a woman

with bright silver hair
lays hands on the lost
forty years after letting me

unbutton her red flannel shirt.
We licked tears of joy
from one another's cheeks

& fed each other cubes
of Gouda as a cold draft
fluttered the blue candle's light.

An old man asks *Are you
coming back?* before I leave
for the last time. The strongest

man in the world gasps
each breath & wants
to be slid into the river

on a raft or given a gun
& left alone a few minutes.
When I say *the arc of a life*

I pantomime a parabola
with my right hand. A girl
dances in Astoria & the boy

who can't keep up
plops onto a cobbler's bench
& then it's 1927, then 1956,

then a grandson the besotted
boy never knew snaps a picture
of his gravestone, remembering

how he took extra care
when he worked there to trim
the long grass of the plot.

With good luck I said.
Ha. I know all my loves
& they me at a glance,

no matter time or pain,
words idiotic or profound.
I'll vanish as I've been vanishing

all along in this gorgeous world.

Christ at the Palace Depression

For all anyone knows, Christ was blue.
Someone said *He shot arrows of dew*.
Does an upper-case "H" do him justice?

He walked among us. The girl with whom
I wove a brocade of blasphemy heals
in His name. Her hair has gone white.

People pay her to pray. Now that no one
remembers George Daynor's ice-blue,
painted-tin icon but me, I prefer Christ

teak-black, slumped in glory atop a cairn
in Seville. Back home, I saw blood run
from His eyes, bead on His arms, puddle

in the gullies of his ribcage. Not even yellow
Christs in Taos bleed as brightly as He did
at the Palace, I swear. Lilies don't root there.

In Him, I mean. The sun has gone dark.
Dwarf pines crowd close. Crows yank meat
from the ribs of a goat.

Russian Vic's Dacha off Mill Road

hunched in a pine copse near the Palace Depression
or what remained of it after bored townspeople, the Headhunters,
        a few dozen after-prom pranksters & the juvenile delinquents

rampaging through the drag-race wee hours of the 1950s
        took their chains, hammers, torches, crowbars & flare-skirted,
happy rage to it. A dead child in Leningrad had hounded Vic

to the swamp where Bill brought him food & a pint
to see him through till the Siloam workday started. No teeth,
        but the hardest gums in history made short work

of the raw onion on break & the cold beets laid on hunks
        of rye for lunch. A great love in Kiev hurled him
where no one anyone remembered had built a chicken coop

& gone belly-up, leaving a hill of lumber, a nail-keg
& three bundles of wire. Snug under the trees, Vic could see
        whenever he wanted the glass-shard, barbed-wire glints

off the blackened Palace in moonlight, sleep a cruel hope,
        grief swelling the red dome of his belly, fingers stroking
the flat stone from the River Ob, where a brother had fallen

through the ice. Only in false dawn did the vaults poured,
gravestones plumbed-up, pints of vodka killed, grave walls
        spaded smooth, root filaments trimmed at long last cudgel

him prone to the pallet where Bill found him snoring each day,
        stove a 55-gallon drum, sink scavenged from Army surplus,
hand-pump dull red, ice box full of wadded shirts. When the last

of the White Russians stowed him on a Black Sea tanker
bound for Varna, Vic could only dream of a *dacha*, never mind
        the wondrous spires & Ford-grille lintels George Daynor

made manifest brick-by-visionary-soup-can. We had a choice
        of myths then—sweat-drenched, drunken-chuckle Atlas
mumbling Slavic work songs or angel-led Appleseed hiking

        from Wall Street to the rectilinear egg capital of the world
& in the immutable way of things, few heeded the gentler voice
        in the permanent wilderness, an illiterate Amos bearing

irrecoverable history from day unto day.

Ode to Newspapers Big as Pizza Boxes

Manhattan/Leesburg/Antigo/Landis Township/Greenwich

You can't any longer whether by whim or design buy *The Village Voice*
          on the way to or from Fairway or Manny's or the Red Apple
whose aisles accommodate but one of the tiny carts though pushy

          babushkas keep doubting it. A friend's father each night read
the *Times'* every squib, but he'd died in a phone booth as his wife
          screamed *Jerome!* into the void, so I didn't witness the deadpan

hilarity with which Jerome sent his kids off to school, backhanding
          huge pages crammed with the inexhaustible idiocy & amazement
of his fellow primates & that's forty years ago already. Like all of us,

          Mr. Walker lived near enough the Palace Depression to see
moonlight glint off the shattered glass in the walls. I'll never know
          whether that really was Roy Wilson chatting up a woman

in a yellow slicker outside a Korean market as damp winter light
          wavered in the wind up Broadway. Why do Koreans run
so many markets there—Upper Broadway, I mean—& why

          are the pyramids of fruit so flawless & fresh? A question
for Spike Lee's orbiting lens to ponder. In Leesburg, The *Times*
          came rolled in the mailbox two days late. At our house,

the *Antigo Daily Journal* spoke of lumber & snow, once one
          or the other parent had peeled the news free of the blue,
onionskin seal. Oh, look: Hilda married Albert & Eastern Star

          enjoyed its biggest installation yet. Lest you wonder, I'd love
to observe my father ponder the *Evening Bulletin*'s box scores
          or trace his right index finger down the *Press's* tide charts

to see how likely the stripers were to run when he next was free
          to cast Into the Sea Isle City surf & I'd love to hear my mother
butcher one more polka on the Lowery under the cuckoo clock

or intone the captions beneath grainy clusters of Brownies
& bizarrely formed cantaloupes, but even lacking such answered
      prayers, the tabloids & broadsheets stacked by the back door

mean decades later I can fail to see from behind the fluttery spread
      of an imaginary *Herald Tribune* or a bitterly actual *Daily News*
the Hudson through the leafed-out poplars & oaks, the big water

      fragrantly bearing barges & tugs the city's monumental hush
muffles enough I can rest enormously alone a block downhill
      from Grant's Tomb & sip coffee hot & silken. In winter,

through the mangled fretwork of trunks & branches, the rolling
      gray water glints beneath the Palisades, but from the tin-can
& shattered concrete threshold of The Palace Depression, you can't

      see the harbor where the Greenwich Tea Party lit the fuse
of revolution, but you can read all about it in the *Journal*'s
      "Our Town" column or the crumbling sheets legend says

Dave Headrick found behind the wainscot in the Teaburner Road parlor—
      or just sit back & inhale low tide in August or November,
no matter what you want or where you think you belong.

"The Last Time I Went Fishing Was The Last Time We Went Fishing"

I don't remember us ever fishing. I remember talking
    about fishing & that time I dropped by the house
        & Denise said (chuckling her Elmer Fudd chuckle)

He's out the spillway thinking straight, whatever that *means*
    so I found you & we killed mosquitoes & smoked up,
        the air all marsh-funk, frog-loud, cattails & sawgrass

silhouetted against the horizon, your rod-tip nodding,
    almost no words. My dad's insurance-payout boat
        with the twin Chrysler 350s? I remember Dave & I

braced at the stern, bouncing bait off the bottom,
    Dad—bald Zorro in a scale-flaked bucket hat—
        cocking an ear, his gorgeous Fenwick a fencing foil

carving Zs in the air, that hairy piston of a right arm
    levering each flounder—thick as his spread hand,
        broad as a dinner plate—into the cooler to slap

a few times while Dave & I clapped & caught nothing.
    I think Dad did that Errol Flynn thing with the rod
        for our benefit. He could be like that sometimes.

It could have been the other Dave that day, but never
    C.J. or Dan. You & I never fished, but I remember
        the time we didn't know we'd left the food & water

home till we pitched the tent after dark, so we hiked
    to Chatsworth at dawn, eating snow, you snarling,
        me ranting innocence, the pines thinning at last,

the cold briny & metallic, then the crossroad & Buzby's,
    the throaty wood stove, the borrowed dime that bought
        Joni's voice, she & Denise pulling up an hour later

for smoky, salty kisses, then the drive home, the feast
of bologna & snack pies I'd begged for, the story of our doings
all down 206 to Buena, the big bend right to Wheat,

the naps in our gimcrack homes. No one could forget that.

Say Yo!

The new casualness had been introducing itself casually, of course, but suddenly its credentials lay everywhere.   John Ashbery

Say *Yo!* & render yourself out-of-date, whether racking
billiard balls or etching a crossbow over your right ear.
Boy, I loved mentholated cigarettes when the rack
at Forcinito's bore a "$5 Carton!" sign & the clerk

ducked her head making change, slid the new
Warlock & the last two *Captain Marvel*s in a bag
& said I should come back soon. Next day,
nifty & keen as a cool breeze, I tossed a tide table

on the counter & a buck on top. Jaunty in white jeans,
I crooked my arm & she took it, crinoline rustling.
A stallion knelt on the worn boards & we mounted,
gazed for a regal moment past the penknives & gum balls

then cantered through the purple heather of my mind.
M'lady Ann, did I not court thee, wisp of Wheat Road,
musk of the Boulevard? 'Twas not that long ago you smoked
a cigarillo on the water slide, tied the damp tails

of my best shirt across your belly & ran the table
at The Oaks as I gobbled half a fried chicken.
Hey, man said I when Melvin slid through the door.
Yo, bro said he, chalking a cue. *Who's that? Cinderella?*

On Plucking a First-Edition *Soul Catcher* Off the Shelf
at Talking Leaves Books, Buffalo, New York

"I don't *believe* in dreams—I *live* in them," I wrote just now elsewhere
          on the continuous page before me. I'd just arisen languidly
from a dream in which Joe handed me the phone across the long,

          oaken table at which we'd sat as he talked to Joni & I ate a bowl
of raspberry Jell-O so as not to seem desperate as everyone knew I was.
          Piecing together from his stoned murmur the plans they'd made,

I hungered to be part of everything, even as I knew I'd see my immutable
          friend soon & no matter what. When at last I pressed the receiver
to my ear, I curled in on myself, hovering my face over the empty bowl,

          so undiluted the pleasure of her voice. Was that Fisher prattling
in the background? Did Greta just bark my name? It took many happy,
          mutually interrupted bursts of talk for Joni to say how good

to be back home. Would I drive Joe & Billy to the Palace Depression
          so we all could play? "Are you kidding?" I said. "I'd cut *grass*
to go play!" "You're my hero," she said. "You've cut square *miles*

          of grass." An hour ago, the cat gazing at me hungry, I wrote,
"Joni's voice runs beneath hearing," a truth inescapable as it is bathetic,
          but I *am* a hero who never fails to bring home from the land

of the dead everything I came for. See? I said "immutable" & meant it.

Just Last Week

I told someone about the time I ran across the field
with Dave, a frisbee flying between us & Dini a few minutes
in the future, waving hello once we'd stopped gliding

over the grass to watch her hit. We'd say *Let's go hit*
then grab rackets, balls & maybe a towel. Telling the tale,
I felt how it felt to fly over the ground with no thought

of feet, how thinking *joy* kills it while the song
the word embalms hums air thick with June bugs, arc lights
furred in the mist, scuff & patter on asphalt, grunt, yelp

& all the way from Brewster Road, glass-pack-rattle-thrum,
radio-squawk, tire-squeal, M-80s in the culvert. Ah, the throb
on gut of ground-stroke & drop! I labored like a roofer in August

to explain. Coffee cold, grin a rictus, my hands quivered
as *light! fearless! free!* & synonyms by the regiment marched
to their doom. We had our kid beds to fall into or haul

to the salt marsh or the pine-duff midden behind any moldered
chicken coop we chose. We ate our mothers' meat loaf,
pocketed their folded tens, breathed our fathers' morning shave,

filled to the sensory brim every bug-crammed, eel-writhing,
biplane-rolled, sweat-salted night, each confession a chance
to glide this way, that way, or no way till someone bearing

our names said *Yes.* Add us up, multiply by an imaginary number
& subtract the facts to equal the home I've built so well I'm not there.

Driving Home

In fifteen minutes I'd go from inside my girl to inside my mother's
        insomniac glare, her paranoia, her terror, her despair & rage
at the most infinitesimal change, but this isn't about that though it ends
        where nothing remains but creek, briars, swamp & two-lane,

tar-seamed concrete the mythic semis no more roar down, road I flew
        to make curfew that summer of joy commonplace as water
but mine to swallow at last, ancient nectar making thirst to sate it.
        Trotting across Park to my father's Jeep, I'd chant what we'd done

without the fear that had aways revved my mind to shrieking—
        my mind, void for seconds at a time—ah, more: She *wanted*
this troll, this gargoyle, this absurd supplicant who'd somehow
        enticed Beatrice to unbraid her black hair, drop the needle

on "I Will" & sing the first verse, Escher print, stack of board games
        & gas meter fluttering in candlelight, cellar a faerie glade—
branch-creak & cricket-chirp, holy oaks & ferns soughing, my love & I
        submerged as we'd been since conception in mortality's sump,

but now *we* would die in some sublime right-now & right-here—
        all this fraught & hyperbolic even then, yet each night good-boy
lies had stolen, I roared past the graveyard where all my dead lay,
        babbling the glory not of "the body" in psalm or sutra, but of two

unrepeatable creatures reborn in one body on a legless sofa & if prayer
        is gratitude realized, I prayed & kept praying as I hove into traffic,
left arm crooked out the window, radio silent, voice freed of intention,
        grace rushing up/pouring down, the hood rising as I careened

across Valley, creaked & squealed around the Wheat bend, vaulted
        the Boulevard, rage to get home the joy incorruptible, beard damp,
fingers fragrant, the milk my mother couldn't give wetting my tongue,
        my father's labor the engine's fire, Body breaking & breaking,

how Mind eats everything no matter anymore, immemorial wind
roaring through the wide-open windows.

The Salt Hay

lined caskets, but who scythed it, bound it, piled the bundles
on the wagons pulled by horses, later by tractors chugging black smoke,
four wagons, six, even eight trundled down the puddled two-tracks
snaking the meadows? To where? Salem? Loaded on flatbed cars
bound for Wilmington, Camden, across the trestle bridge
to Philadelphia where the carpenters tucked handfuls of hay
between the casket walls & the satin tacked into pentagonal
pillows so the body would rest unbruised & dignified?
Who owned the land barely land, spongy, squelching, tidal punk
a pall from Shiloh south, horsefly clouds through the windless summers?
Who rowed the punts tied to the dock tumbled over the brackish creek?
Who crabbed off the bridge? Who worked the kerosene heaters,
skinned the minks & muskrats, plucked the woodcock clean?
Who ate the eels roasting on the rusted freezer grate? Who drove
to the Egg Harbor icehouse for the blocks half-melted
by sunset, cream soda frosty, catfish briny, numbers totted up,
moon full though faint overhead, a damp shiver in the air,
the sun squatting white & huge or bitter orange on the bay?

Horticulture

Because Judy had given me for Christmas a lumpen pot
  she'd pinched & baked right in her kitchen, I tried
my first African Violet just after New Year's. The cat nosed

  its furry leaves, so I braced a two-by-six where fan belts
had hung when the place was a gas station. That spring,
  I dug up a fern at Parvin's & Billy rinsed a #10 can

of sauerkraut, drilled holes in the bottom & scooped it
  full of Magic Mix. People gave me stuff all the time.
I started a potato in the pot my mother's geraniums died in,

  then hung in white pots eye-bolted to the ceiling a yam,
spider plants, ivy & an aloe Judy had coaxed back to life.
  The miraculous fertilizer had just come to market,

so I had a jungle up there. What sudden leaves! Then again,
  I burned a ficus & a miniature lemon tree. Billy & Judy
taught us all, having turned the bungalow whose windows

  spilled amber light on the lot behind Williams Liquors
into the Land of Cockaigne & when they threw the place
  open in spring, the rustle & rattle of dappled leaves

mingled with the tar-seamed beat of Route 47, our happily
  heedless chatter & everything lost to memory or plucked
from it—a faerie tune melting the iron night of winter.

Billy on Leave in Alaska

       squinted in the tent's befogged gloom, lips pursed
round the joint, pinkie up in stoner salute, trooper hat
       tilted back, fur-lined earflaps sticking out frozen—

no surprise he'd hike so far on his first leave
       out of Fort Richardson, scribble the gloating note
to those who hadn't broken free enough to do

       something other than think themselves wizened
at twenty, working shit jobs in the flatlands, humping
       scavenged furniture from cellar to flat to insulated

chicken coop to dorm room to attic to cellar again.
       Hear his reedy voice. Hear him giggle at visions
made real. Hear him dote on comic books, hunch over

       the receiver like a safecracker till the stolen Jensens
made our sternums hum, tie his hair back when the poker
       got serious. Here's where "years later" usually comes,

but Billy deserves to stay in Alaska, chewing the dried salmon
       the guide sold him, sipping whiskey for warmth, naming
for his new friends the mountains they see out the tent's mouth.

The Invention of Gunpowder

Driving west, we compare barbecue-beef sandwiches to ox roast,
me greasy at one of the innumerable picnics, my wife
on her sweaty way to Whippy Dip. An English Ford
rattles down the two-track. The smoke of zapped bees

curls above the workers whacking buckets of orange golf balls
into the weedy heat. The nights are brief & endless. One solstice,
a few of us camped at Bass River, eating psilocybin at whim,
aroma of salt & firelight, sexual fumbling, visionary laughter

at nothing. On the bluff, a hand-sized hunk of silken granite
good for skinning mastodons. What lives here? I don't mean
dreams, even dreams of the Japanese migrants who laid out
a wedding feast of raw everything that time. Strangled whiff

of cordite, the marksmanship medal pinned to the blue shirt.
Rest is real as work & food more so, soaking through paper plates.

Merit Badge

In a corner
Of the same tent a small boy in a coat
Sobs and sobs…   Allen Grossman

Mike's transistor crackles a mystery
from 1940. He says, "My pop loves
this show." It's 1965, but I don't say so.
His mess kit floats between us.
After Kirchner paired-up the troop

for bare-knuckle bouts round the fire,
my three uphill punches landed in the air
beneath Mike's chin, so he kicked my legs
from under me. Then the rain came again.
Lard-ass me. Swamp Thing him. I rattle

the dead flashlight. The radio sells scrapple.
Mike can't read a compass. I can't swim.
The boxing bored Kirchner, so no one
earned dinner, but you can't expect better
when you fail to lash a lean-to, fail to orienteer,

fail to work flint & tinder, fail to march
by the left flank march by the left flank march
in the black rain that rivers among the pines.
The pain in my bladder is biblical. Kirchner hates
what pathetic excuses we are. I like *Combat!*

Mike says *The Gallant Men* look like his pop's
old platoon. I can't explain Boy Scouts
to my son. "Why did you do what you hated?"
What an adventure the soaked sleeping bag,
its plaid flannel, its leaky, vulcanized shell,

the stink of boy-sweat & mildewed canvas.
I split the sleeve of saltines my mother zipped
in a bank-deposit pouch. The organ deepens

the mystery. Mike gives me his canteen
& I give him the crackers, a slice of cheese,

half the chocolate bar I've been hoarding,
but the radio dies & the rain goes on,
all of us way too old to want our mothers
to come for us as they've always promised
to come carry us out of the all-night rain.

III

Names & Places

In 1945, everything burned
in many places. A boy joined

the Future Farmers of America.
Another dubbed himself "Butch"

& was Butch to everyone—
even children & grandchildren—

from then on. No one knows
how many souls went

from dailiness to shadow
on various stone walls

& benches. I forget this
for years at a time.

I refuse to name the places
where everything burned.

Blossoms unfold
each spring everywhere.

Photographs make it seem
normal. The boy never farmed.

His mother cooked chicken
& dumplings whenever he asked.

99% of the souls ever to live
never ate dumplings. Spirochetes

are sometimes the price
of ecstasy. An ex-Marine

named Jimmy in a place
I refuse to name gimped

behind a lawn mower
eight hours a day & drank

a quart of vodka every Saturday,
saying *Okinawa didn't kill me,*

so what's a little hooch?
Butch was a happy man,

especially brushing lacquer
on a balsa-wood model

or pitching woo (though Anita)
needed no convincing) or tuning

the shortwave to the BBC.
Sorrow isn't enough. Butch knew

what "to bayonet" meant
& liked to pantomime it.

Chicken farms by the score
or the million: ash. Happiness

is possible. Love seizes
the content & the bitter

in nameless places everywhere.

Beets

Beets was the only man at the Maplewood
could hold the table on Dyke Night & not
piss off Maxy & her crew when he bawled
"Dyke up!" after a missed shot. A dime bought
a game then, the beer a quarter & cold,
roast beef piled three inches high on the Kaiser.
We had legends & letters—Beets pitched woo
hard as Feller, charmed two wives to Estelle Manor,
where the jive crumbled fast as the week-old bread
Beets made his daily gift to the larder. Born for the heat
of the bar in winter, happiest reading Thomas Wolfe
past closing, feet crossed near the Wedgewood,
calling "Hey! Listen to this beauty of a thing!"
as Jack & Pam swept up, he'd left the war
as far behind as anyone had, which even Maxy
would tell you means about an inch. Beets wrote
a fine hand. If you weren't a wife sailing envelopes
into the fire, you'd treasure whatever he sent.

What Lola Means to Me

after Linda Lee Harper

A genii who once blew a ferret into pink mist
with the birdshot double-load Mister kept to pepper
the ass of any fool tried to steal so much as a rusty nail—
Lola Bank granted no wish ever, work the thing
& lucky to have it & squat in your own shit

for a year if you don't like it. I did like it & learned it
long after no one alive had ever seen a ferret raise up
on hind legs at the end of the dock Lola & Mister
shared with his cousins. Grandma Bank owned that end
of Port Elizabeth & her wish was law well beyond family.

No one knew what a ferret was till Mister read the article
in *Collier's* after concluding his wife hadn't shot a weasel
or a cat. We worked like mules, air so thick in summer
you could scrape a kitchen knife down your arm & salt
your food with what flaked off. We had water rats

& dogs who loved killing them. Lola was Ma Barker
only tall, black as creosote & the real mayor of Tuckahoe,
Port Elizabeth & far away as Brotmanville. The dogs tore
rats & raccoons apart & bloodied one another doing it.
Not old enough yet to work, I found a wood-spoked

wheel one day far back in the meadows & brought it to her.
She touched it, nodded, glanced at Mister & said *So that's
where she is* & waved me home. It's not memory
if you're living it. It doesn't mean anything. It's heat & salt
& hatred of endings though that's what happens.

Civil Service, Soldiers' Home

Pay & Benefits

$2.50 an hour to start,
sick days accrued from date of hire,
five vacation days the first year
provided you pass probation.

Translation: Don't piss off Joe C, Kenny,
Clog, Twatsky, The General, Mother,
Main Office Marge, or The Platypus
& you've got not only a job,

but in twenty-five years a blowjob
of a pension, guaranfuckingteed.

Intangibles

French toast, state-warehouse margarine & Mrs. Butterworth's.
#10 cans of cling peaches, mandarin oranges, white cherries.
Two-foot cylinders of bologna, liverwurst & Canadian bacon.
Loaves of bread warm from the State School.
Hot roast beef sandwiches, mashed potatoes & gravy
whenever Manny owed Joe C a favor.

*

Joe C all day in the break room
in ironed work greens
& buffed Red Balls.

*

A keg in the bed of Kenny's pickup
on morning break.

*

The Clog & Jimmy Show:
Kiss my shiny black ass, Clog!
Suck my Semper Fi dick, Jimmy!

Chin-to-chin yelling
till Sam wedged between
so one could say *Shit, Sam.*
It was just getting good.

*

Sam laying rubber every break
to tend his wife, crumpled
by multiple sclerosis, Clog saying
He waters her like a potted plant.

*

Sam knowing what was what.
When he said stop or go
you stopped or went
because Sam Esposito said so.

Natalie

The med tech who drove a Capri
& loved Joey, horses & Bruni's meatball subs.

Her green polka-dot dress.
Her dabs of *Eau de 1973.*

Her up on the examination room counter,
swinging her legs, chatting & chatting,

gulping her big gulping laugh,
me rolling around on the little black stool,

glimpsing & glimpsing the silken yeehah scarlet
nearly-nothing any true religion would forgive me wanting

to tug down with my two hooked pinkies.
Oh the whimsical tent-fly to Natalie.

Oh the crinkling Dr. Seuss trap-door
to the aromatic secret I thought the gist of Natalie.

Bruno

The summer after Nixon saved me,
I worked the grounds crew with Joey & Balls,
afternoon break a beer apiece & a joint

of the bad Mexican Joey scored
for ten an ounce in Buena Vista.
Oh boy, did we cool off in the gazebo

the summer after I'd flown into Da Nang
a thousand times. No matter how smart
all my school made me, I was infantry

at the pre-induction physical.
Now I was high in the Soldiers' Home gazebo
& about to get higher: strolling through the Grove

came Bruno in creased whites, corncob clenched
between teeth pearly as albino mussel shells.
We shook our soul-shakes, said our *que pasas*

& lit the *chiba* white boys weren't up to
unless they got *educated*, lived some *life*,
maybe did a tour in the Delta,

which *learned* you, motherfucker, no matter who
& dope the least of it. But Bruno knew
we weren't just any white boys. We spoke

Street Rican for bedrock truths like *You are fecund
as a harvest moon, my sweet* & *Sir, your sexual proclivities
appall me.* We didn't sweep glass from the city-park courts

& hold our own for nothing. Joey was Pepito
in high school though he—or at least his father—
was Sicilian. Balls was seriously white

though he swung-clomped a leg his dirt bike
mangled in a cow field near Pitman. I had a fat beard
with gray in it & could talk any talk, oh yeah.

Anyway, we smoked up. Got blind. Whoosh.
Oh boy. Bruno left & we stayed & stayed.
Then we swept the sidewalk, clipped the hedge

& trimmed the wisteria behind Unit One.
Though I told Balls I'd seen God,
I hadn't, but I did see the concrete

& what I swept from it
& the grass I swept it onto
& the black-bristled push-broom shooshing,

my hands & arms brown & undulating,
wet in the white heat of that day in skunk-weed,
pitch-pine, safe-white-boy New Jersey—

& that seeing stayed seen.

Shimmy Shimmy Ko-Ko-Bop

...Ladies shimmy/at Jimmy in waves.   Ted Berrigan

Once shed of his painter's whites,
Jimmy glistened lotion-smooth in fake
alligator loafers. Marlboro-tipped,
get-some-action vodka sipped, he slipped

out the Maintenance back door to his blue
& beat Chrysler. Somewhere around 1985,
someone admonished me about "glisten"
& "gleam" & I did give that bullshit

almost a minute's thought, so call
me permanently fair. Waves are wan
in Berrigan & often his clock strikes 5:15.
Jimmy worked the joint on Wheat where all

the ladies glistened & gleamed. He liked
the sequins, the conga hips, the red, red lips.

They Could Have Had Something

They could have had something,
Dottie & him. He was white, she black,

which mattered to both of them,
but that's a guess in both directions

after all this time. She was his work wife,
he the husband laying out hoagies

& chips (& cleaning up!) once
or twice a week. Such good

talks! No guesswork there.

Breakfast at the Woodstown Diner

Jimmies remain jimmies at the Woodstown Diner,
so the cool, clear day relaxes. A Greek omelet,
home fries, toast & coffee they must perk
to conjure scrapple like this. No more
Atlantic City Press, but the tiny weekly
does feature cranberry rakes in the classifieds.
I like being "Hon," especially since the "Hon"
the waitress uses on the others lacks
the wholesome fondness, not to mention
the fetching smile my Hon-ness inspires.
The ice cream—peach, please—will not
be as it was, but the jimmies, as I've said,
remain permanent. If this were the right year,
I'd toss a few silver dollars on the counter
& give this Tina a jaunty, two-fingered salute
as I bop to the door. Too bad they drained
Malaga Lake & tore down the skating rink.
I still bop. Tina still smiles, folding the bills
into her apron pocket with everything else.

IV

Poem Beginning With a Line From Fernando Pessoa

(as Àlvaro de Campos)

As long as fate permits, I'll go on smoking,
whether Trish's father's pipe, packed with no-brand rag
on the Red House porch after the Big Snow
or the Faber-Castell #2B with which I mime
Camels & strike-anywhere matches or the Winstons

that dropped into the tray once I'd inserted two quarters
& pulled the knob & heard the rattly clanking
(remember stripping the cellophane, peeling the foil,
tapping the pack on the first knuckle of the left hand,
lighting the first fresh one up, hunching back

into the rain to pump a dollar of hi-test to quiet
the valve-clatter Joe said he'd investigate but never did?)
or the candy Luckies or the cheroots that fit
the West I gazed upon out the train window,
sleepless, forlorn & heartbroken as only

a 25-year-old can convince himself he is
or truly is with Sacramento the next stop
& home in his pockets. Hold the butt
lit-end down & watch the smoke furl
between the fingers. You can really think then.

October Cold Rain Refusing

Hot this month, cold rain refusing to break loose.
Nice to think rain can decide or forget or hoard

crimson leaves till one morning that may not come,
damp heat factitious as the swollen parotid

or a high-C shrieked a full eight bars, whisper
becomes roar in seconds, dust mud under the dead

peony. Nature's will & perfect discernment a necessary
cliché, nothing idiosyncratic about it— "The universe

revolves around me!" as we say in our house,
joking at the human—or at least American—

need to think the Purpose from primordial
bacteria to right now the satisfaction of our hunger,

knowing perfectly well the universe doesn't know
from revolution. Meanwhile, eating has never yet

stopped, but you don't need an alimentary canal
to know that. "Tomorrow is promised to no one,"

goes the cliché, but it's necessary fun not to believe it.

Oh, Those Summer Mornings in the Days of Empire

Teele Square, Somerville, Massachusetts, 1978

She loved zucchini quiche & iced ale,
        but that spinach thing, your specialty?
                Back to the Garden you went, Adam,

& don't you forget it, the curled blue
        kitchen linoleum cool the next morning,
                peanut omelet for her, yogurt for you,

cutoffs & t-shirts wadded in the corner,
        & oh, the bliss of the Union Square Sears!
                The valve-clattering drive to the guarantee

of frigid evaporation as banks of TVs
        blared the immaculate Sox! You both ate
                & gabbed all summer, nipping knees

& salty necks browned in Gloucester,
        oiled at Walden Pond, sizzled to sopping
                on the fire escape & landings & every square

millimeter of that drape-free flat, salved
        (just maybe, please God) past midnight
                as Art & Bob's blared. The *Globe* said

Egypt (or maybe Norway) had vaporized
        all its progress (as "Ozymandias," history
                & pre-history foretold), a sublimation

then well underway in several spheres
        of influence—um, nation-states—er, missile-
                bristling topographies of collective psychosis,

just the usual mishmashing doohickeys
        of laughter & harvests & weaponry scrabbling
                lethally down the misty slopes of thingamabob

whatchamacallits permanently harmonic
      in their forever aromatic grandiloquence. Hmm.
            How'd this come to this? Oh, yes, that asbestos-

shingled three-decker down whose steps
      you bounded to Mass. Ave., sweating rivers.
            Stoned, she said, "Why's Norway Norway?"

Naked & un-toweled post-shower, you said,
      "What?" Wet & red as a boiled lobster, she said,
            "Because in Scotland it's Way Nor'!" Oh to fall

out like that! Bony asses crunching, nothing
      between skin & city but rooms unchanged
            since maybe 1930. What a sniveling asshole

that Shelley, revivified in the huge book
      propped on your knees in the bus & two trains
            to work & back. She loved hearing you bellow

"Get a job, Percy!" Too hot, but you baked
      & on Sundays went for the papers & double-dip
            peach cones (with chocolate jimmies!) at Joey's.

Apollo

Tilted at a reentry angle, the capsule
demonstrates how cramped & primitive
the Apollo years. Kids peal how small
the astronauts must have been,

the docent urging awe at their courage,
especially when it came to squeezing
food from toothpaste tubes. Best not
to ask too much of ones so young.

Science is serious fun & the capsule
looks real. Millions of imaginations
thrilled to simulations & wee-hour
transmissions from inside the speck

hurtling to the animated moon.
Look at the heat shield atmospheric
friction chipped & blackened!
They've propped the hatch open.

This thing bobbed on the open sea.
Engineers reasoned each bit from nothing.

Some Random Issues

Things are so much more random now,
what with all the issues everyone has,
especially when going off on someone
(or having been gone off on)
or going off of what someone says
without first feeling them or her or him
so no words get put in mouths—I mean,
what you put out comes back on you,
but to stray from my lane a second,
let me pull your coat about this random thing
because it looks to this old head like memes
are another thing, right? (Memes & a zillion
more things every flip of the lid, but hang
with me now) Scope the ten-gallon
Pharrell Williams rocked when he first got big.
Think "Who 'dat?" all you want, but dude
looked like a miniature Tom Mix, you feel me?
Whitest cat in the movies till Gene Autry's
bleached-out serials where everyone sang
in saddles. Dang, I came up when it was dope
to wear a coonskin cap, but phew, Pharrell
needed a new haberdasher & still does,
last I looked. Hate me for harshing so hard,
but every tick-tock makes my home in the land
of Maypo more freaky, country where one stored
one's milk in the Frigidaire & handkerchiefs
had yet to become Kleenex. Neutrons once
were never random. Electrons orbited. Old hat?
Damn straight. No way "gamma" could ever
modify "knife"? Nah. Those bad boys heal
the sick every minute. Notice a proton
or it isn't? The universe no longer "the"?
Everything nearly nothing, no matter mass?
Grok *that*, dude. Can't make that shit up.

Another Naïve Poem

Even after all that? The pen in which Rex
snuffled my snow-suited armpit or the scatter
of tomato stakes once the snow made cold mud
of everything from back step to tool shed all the way
to roofless chicken coop, wooden bucket & crowbar?
Even after jalousie windows, wicker chair, the hat woven
from sweetgrass, a pane of green cellophane in the crown?
Everything has swerved near again. May I crawl up the stairs

& lean against what wall there is under the eave? May I pluck
burrs from my socks & pick blackberries for the cream & scrub
the tiny spikes from the cucumbers? No? After all that's happened
I should know not to ask, should swallow this sour bolus of *So what?*
& trudge on, good soldier, good burgher, good Stoic, good man & true?
Look: I've put the pencil down. Both hands lie open.

After Driving Through the Holland Tunnel

we'd window-shopped antiques
on MacDougal, shivering
in our pea coats. Have I

told you this already?
We pointed uptown & down,
bought a newspaper & a map

from a man bundled behind
a green plywood counter.
We climbed five steps

into a wine bar where wine
threaded one of the cheeses
they brought on a board

bearing an apple, a paring knife
& a miniature baguette, a word
among many on the menu

unknown & therefore worldly.
I've probably said this already.
We ordered a bottle of Lancer's

& they brought it—my beard,
her mass of black hair,
the way we manipulated

cigarettes & our having come
to nestle in The Village—navel
of the world—on a commonplace

winter night all the verification
we'd need forever. Frosty taillights
drifted past our window booth

& people blowing out fog.
We fed each other & drank
the best wine we'd ever drunk,

so elemental I can't believe
I haven't told you what joy
I've had being here all this time.

Ice Cream Sandwich

Consider how the ice cream sandwich obliterates
the memory of all previous ice cream sandwiches.

Consider the ice cream itself, the skin
that grew during months of storage.

Consider how each bite threads fault lines
through both chocolate rectangles.

Consider the blast-furnace day that shot
the ice cream sandwich from the freezer.

Consider the miracle of the freezer & the ice cream
& the stars, too, the stars that aren't stars, but galaxies.

Consider the frozen river in this photograph,
how blue the ice on the granite wall.

Consider how a twenty-ton granite shelf sheared
off the wall in August, 1886 & killed no one.

Consider all the picnics, parasols
& straw boaters in the woods & fields then.

Consider how the moment the woman in the hat
for which untold birds died dipped her spoon

in the wooden bucket, ice cream had bestowed bliss
on the human tongue for a thousand years.

Consider the desire for a second ice cream sandwich
the first inspires & how the first thought is "No,

too much sweet" & the second is "Why the hell not?"
Consider how after the first bite all thoughts hum

"Heaven" till the ice cream sandwich is gone.

In the Pines

How can you make a case for yourself
before an ocean of trees, or standing
waist-deep in the river?…   Jim Harrison, "Cabin Poem"

In a canvas rucksack, he totes grief's rootstock & the overripe,
avocado-ish fruit of the go-along-get-along tree (*Caecus timore*)

deep in the pines, his *carpe diem* friend setting the pace along
the packed-sand trail, rumor of river scenting the Venus-hot air,

horsefly crowns of thorns bouncing on both their heads,
sweat coursing down their crisping torsos & crimson legs,

sneakers damp & flexing & there comes a clearing
near a river bend where they drop everything & step naked

into willow-hooped shade, find the channel neck-deep & narrow
& bob up & under an uncounted span of cool, purling bliss

among water-skaters, white butterflies, moss & watercress,
echoic blurts of gut-bucket gratitude without end.

Notes

Many of these poems mention altered, obscure, or vanished places, technologies, food ways, and cultural artifacts, as well as numerous adventurers (whether bearing given names or aliases) in love, rage, absurdity, grief, and exaltation. Like all poems, these suffer the inescapable flaws of their maker yet in every syllable seek to ensoul what they say and to do so with blinding clarity, no matter how hermetic.

A number of these poems dramatize details concerning The Palace Depression, a recently restored instance of Americana located in Vineland, New Jersey. RoadsideAmerica.com provides an accurate-as-far-as-it-goes account: "Completed on Christmas Day, 1932, the Palace of Depression was an eighteen-spired, pastel-colored castle" built by an eccentric visionary named George Daynor. Using a variety of found materials (he particularly favored using automobile grilles for doorway arches), Daynor constructed his "'Home of Junk'...to show that the Great Depression was beatable."

By his own testimony, "Daynor was a former Alaska gold miner. He accumulated a fortune, then lost it all in the Wall Street crash of 1929. With only four dollars in his pocket, he was guided to New Jersey by an angel," and on his first day, bought four marshy acres on the corner of Mill Road and Landis Avenue. "Realizing that George had the proper can-do attitude and was good with his hands, the angel provided him with the basic design for his Palace...He ate frogs, fish, rabbits and squirrels during the three years it took to build..."

Accounts differ. The angel may have visited Daynor once he'd already bought the land (sight unseen) and had fallen asleep in the bed of a junked pickup. He may have had seven dollars in his pocket. The swampy tract on which he built the Palace may have been the last in the area to be sold for a dollar an acre. Daynor may have been 104 when he died in 1964, but maybe not.

I have dim childhood memories of poking around the Palace's ruins with my father. Almost certainly, he and his brothers were among the 500,000 visitors who paid admission to "The Strangest House in the World" during the thirty years George Daynor gave tours.

When speaking of the Palace of Depression, local residents omit "of." In making the poems that mention the Palace, I've altered geography as needed.

"Billy on Leave in Alaska" (p. 42) remembers William Ruff.

"In the Pines" (p. 73) remembers David Graham.

"'The Last Time I Went Fishing is the Last Time We Went Fishing'" (p. 34) is for Joe Freeman.

"Russian Vic's Dacha off Mill Road" (p. 30) remembers Russian Vic (a.k.a Big Vic) and William Ingling.

About the Author

John Repp is a writer, folk photographer, and digital collagist living in Erie, Pennsylvania. He grew up along the Blackwater Branch of the Maurice River in the Pine Barrens region of southern New Jersey, a time and place that has nourished his artistic practice for fifty years. His twenty books and chapbooks of poetry and fiction include *The Soul of Rock & Roll: Poems Acoustic, Electric & Remixed, 1980-2020* (Broadstone Books); *Fat Jersey Blues*, winner of the Akron Poetry Prize from the University of Akron Press; and *Thirst Like This*, winner of the Devins Award from the University of Missouri Press.

Repp's website features much more information about his work, influences, and obsessions: www.johnreppwriter.com.